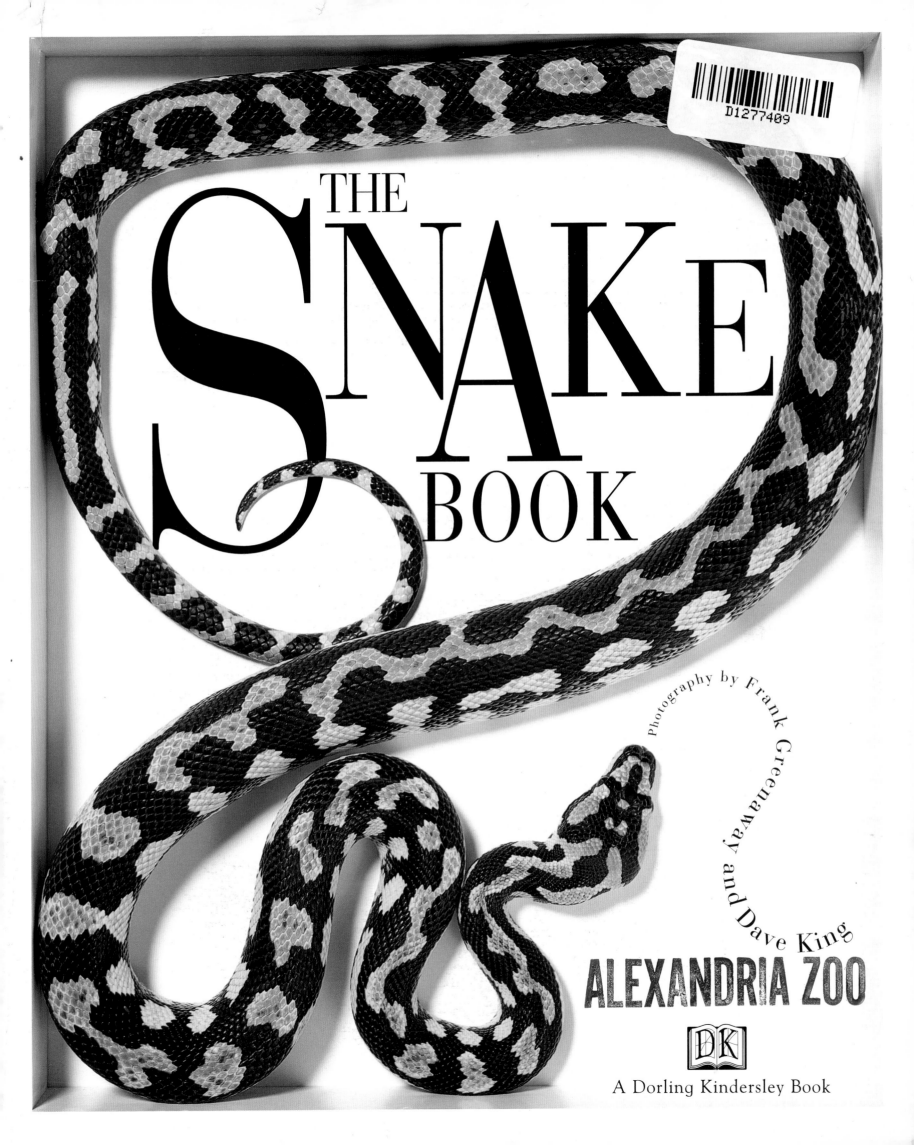

THE SNAKE BOOK

Photography by Frank Greenaway and Dave King

ALEXANDRIA ZOO

DK

A Dorling Kindersley Book

Introduction

Snakes have the simplest body shape of all creatures. Yet they are

highly specialized and efficient hunting machines, fully deserving

their reputation as fearsome predators. Each of the nearly 3,000

different species has adapted its basic design to suit its particular

habitat perfectly, be it a hot, dry desert or a muddy swamp.

The result is an immense variety of colors, shapes, and

textures, and a wide range of killing techniques, from

simply swallowing prey whole, or squeezing

the life from a victim, to

injecting lethal venom

through sharp fangs.

Turn the page for a

really close-up look

– if you dare.

DK

Dorling Kindersley

LONDON, NEW YORK, SYDNEY, DELHI, PARIS,
MUNICH and JOHANNESBURG

Written and edited by
Mary Ling
and Mary Atkinson

Managing Art Editor
Jane Horne

Art Editor
Ivan Finnegan

Designer
Piers Tilbury

DTP Designer
Nicola Studdart

US Editor
Camela Decaire

Production
Ruth Cobb

Consultant
Colin McCarthy

First American Edition, 1997
10 9 8 7 6 5 4 3 2 1

First paperback edition, 2000

Published in the United States by
Dorling Kindersley Publishing, Inc.
95 Madison Avenue
New York, NY 10016

See our complete catalog at: **www.dk.com**

A catalog record for this book is available from the Library of Congress.

ISBN 0-7894-6068-8

Color reproduction by Colourscan
Printed and bound in Italy by L.E.G.O.

Dorling Kindersley would like to thank Mark O'Shea
and Marc Ormond for their advice and
for supplying the snakes in this book.

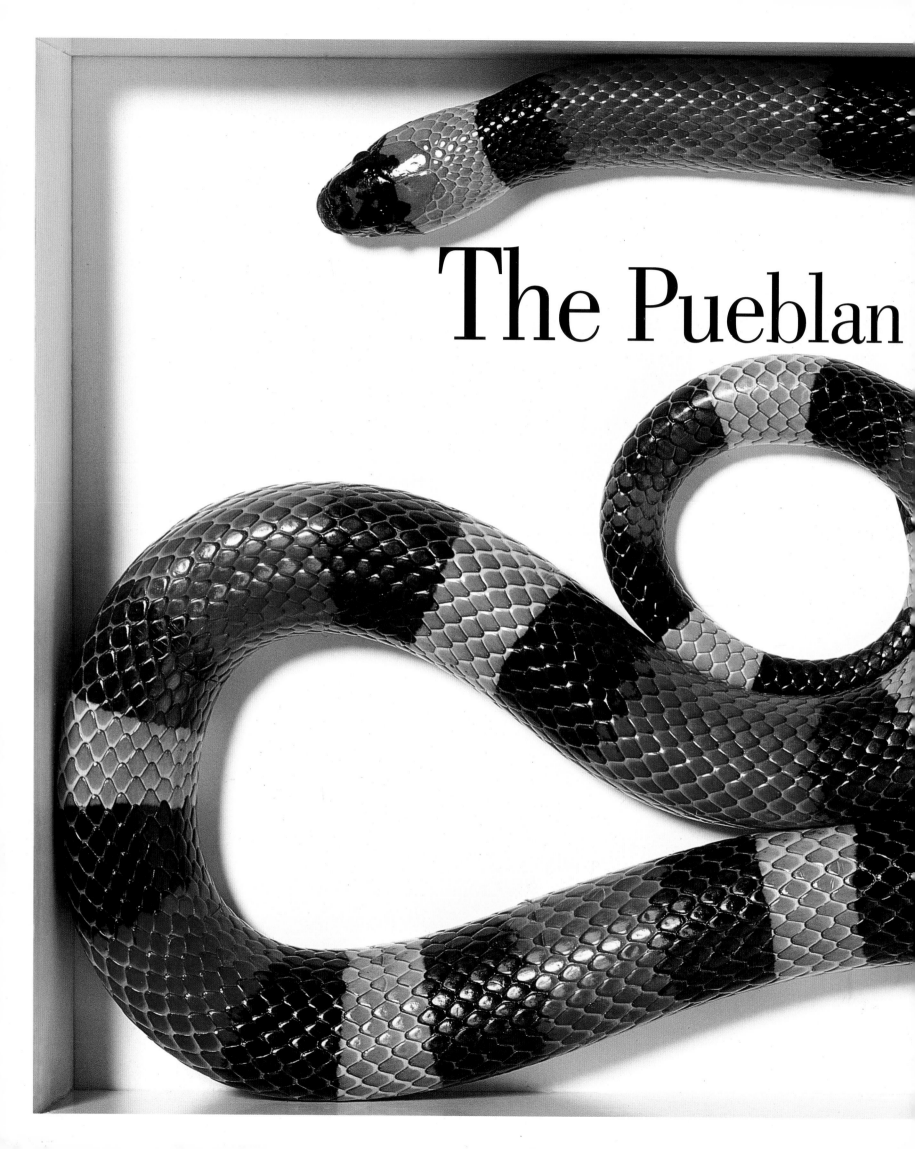

The Pueblan

milk snake disappears ...in a streak of black, red, and cream. For a split second, these bold rings of color disguise the snake's shy nature and startle predators – time enough to escape danger so the snake can resume its own merciless hunt.

It was once believed that milk snakes enter barns to dine on cows' milk. In fact, they're merely hunting mice.

The rainbow boa
is best known for its glittering color. Every scale has a microscopic ridge that acts like a tiny prism, shimmering as the snake slithers over the ground. At night, the rainbow boa hunts small mammals and birds. Heat-sensing pits in its upper jaws detect the body heat of prey, allowing it to home in with deadly accuracy, even on the darkest, starless night.

The horned viper

is perfectly adapted to the desert sands that are its home. To escape the wild extremes of temperature, or when preparing an ambush, it rapidly vibrates its body until it is submerged up to its eyes in sand. There it waits, virtually invisible. Special peaked scales protrude like horns over the viper's eyes so the drifting sand never prevents a clear lookout from its bunker. Should it be spotted by a hungry enemy, such as a fennec fox, it rubs together the serrated scales that run along its body. The rasping sound instantly informs the predator that to attack would be to risk a fatal injection of venom as the viper flicks forward its deadly fangs.

The everglades rat snake

is so named for its fondness for rats and other rodents. It is astonishingly athletic when pursuing prey, climbing high into tall trees or swiftly slithering from branch to building. When the hunt is successful, the snake wraps its wide, outstretched mouth around its prey.

The hinges of its jaw flick apart, then two rows of curved, sharp teeth push the victim along, deep into its throat.

The Californian king

snake ...

has a penchant for

eating other snakes – they're

the perfect shape to swallow!

It is even prepared to take

on the deadly rattlesnake.

Immune to the poison

of the rattler, the king snake has little

to fear. Californian king snakes are

polymorphic – some are black and white, others

are brown and cream; some have stripes, others have rings.

The reticulated python is a giant among serpents, sometimes growing to be 33 ft (10 m) of powerful muscle. The constrictor holds its prey tight in gripping jaws, then coils around its struggling victim's body to immobilize it. With each exhale of the victim, the python relentlessly coils tighter, squeeeeeeeeeeezing all life from it, yet barely breaking a bone.

The
boa constrictor
lives among trees in South American rain forests. It's not a picky eater, enjoying a diet of birds, eggs, and various mammals.

Unlike most snakes, which lay eggs, the female boa constrictor gives birth to live baby boas.

She finds a sheltered spot, such as

the hollow of a tree, where up to 50

young can safely wiggle

into the world.

The long,
sleek cribo
of Mexico and

Central and South America

is slim enough to slither into a

warm burrow in search of a tasty meal.

It has no venom, but it can either constrict its

prey or take it and, with a whiplash

action, pin it against a rock

or a burrow wall.

The suffocating creature has

little hope of recovering before it is

swallowed alive. Although the victim soon dies,

it will take the snake about a week

to digest its meal.

The mangrove snake hisses

and rears up in anger

as it vents its fury on any

predator not already warned off the attack

by its bold black-and-yellow colors. This venomous

inhabitant of Asian rain forests hunts at night, scaling giant trees

in search of food. Captured prey is held at the back of its mouth, where

sharp teeth break its skin. Toxic saliva starts the digestion process when

grooves in the snake's piercing rear fangs deliver deadly

poison deep into the victim's body.

THE CAT SNAKE

hunts at night. Its catlike eyes are well equipped to glimpse even the smallest movement as it searches for its prey, gliding through vines and branches high in the canopy of the rain forest.

Silently it stretches from tree to tree, its length supported by the wide scales on its underbelly. Its forked tongue flickers to detect the scent of a bat or sleeping bird and, in a flash, sharp fangs inject a deadly poison. The cat snake rests in the day, comfortably twined around a branch,

perfectly camouflaged.

RATTLESNAKES

AS LEGEND HAS IT, THE ominous tail buzz of the rattler warns cowboy and cattle alike of imminent danger. Few predators would dare ignore a rattlesnake rearing up its body and furiously shaking the bold black-and-white rattle on the tip of its tail. One bite from this small but highly venomous creature quickly kills its victim.

Looking and feeling just like fine velvet, this extraordinarily beautiful snake hangs headfirst from branches in the Australian rain forest. There it quietly waits, ready to snatch a passing meal of fruit bat, bandicoot, or opossum.

Its dense colors make it almost invisible at night, but in sunlight, every color of the rainbow sparkles from the iridescent scales of the amethystine python.

SNAKE STATISTICS

1. PUEBLAN MILK SNAKE (*Lampropeltis triangulum campbelli*)
Distribution: Mexico
Food: mainly small rodents and reptiles
Method of hunting: a constrictor
Length: can reach 3 ft (1 m)

2. RAINBOW BOA (*Epicrates cenchria*)
Distribution: South America
Food: small mammals and birds
Method of hunting: a constrictor
Length: can exceed 6.5 ft (2 m)

3. AFRICAN DESERT HORNED VIPER (*Cerastes cerastes*)
Distribution: North Africa and the Middle East
Food: mainly rodents and reptiles
Method of hunting: venomous bite (deadly to humans)
Length: usually reaches 2 ft (60 cm)

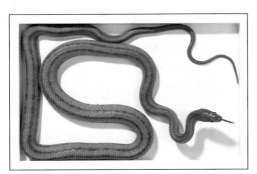

4. EVERGLADES RAT SNAKE (*Elaphe obsoleta rossalleni*)
Distribution: southern Florida, US
Food: rats and other rodents
Method of hunting: a constrictor
Length: can reach 6.5 ft (2 m)

5. CALIFORNIAN KING SNAKE (*Lampropeltis getula californiae*)
Distribution: western US and Mexico
Food: eggs, birds, rodents, and reptiles
Method of hunting: a constrictor
Length: can reach 6.5 ft (2 m)

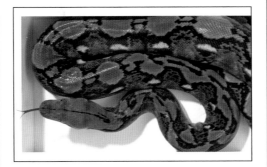

6. RETICULATED PYTHON (*Python reticulatus*)
Distribution: Southeast Asia
Food: mammals, birds, large lizards, and snakes
Method of hunting: a constrictor (can kill humans)
Length: longest recorded snake, reaching 32 ft (10 m)

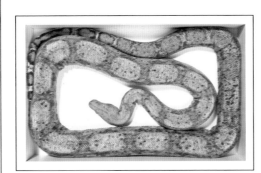

7. BOA CONSTRICTOR (*Boa constrictor*)
Distribution: Mexico, Central and South America
Food: mammals and birds
Method of hunting: a constrictor
Length: can reach 20 ft (6 m)

8. BLACK-TAILED CRIBO (*Drymarchon corais*)
Distribution: Mexico, Central and South America
Food: birds, amphibians, reptiles, and small mammals
Method of hunting: a constrictor
Length: can reach 8 ft (2.5 m)

9. MANGROVE SNAKE (*Boiga dendrophila melanota*)
Distribution: Southeast Asia
Food: eggs, birds, reptiles, and small mammals
Method of hunting: venomous bite and constriction
Length: can reach 8 ft (2.5 m)

10. GREEN CAT SNAKE (*Boiga cyanea*)
Distribution: Southeast Asia
Food: tree-dwelling amphibians and reptiles
Method of hunting: venomous bite and constriction
Length: can reach 5.2 ft (1.6 m)

11. WESTERN DIAMONDBACK RATTLESNAKES (*Crotalus atrox*)
Distribution: southwestern US and northern Mexico
Food: birds and rodents
Method of hunting: venomous bite (deadly to humans)
Length: can exceed 7 ft (2.1 m)

12. AMETHYSTINE PYTHON (*Morelia amethistina*)
Distribution: New Guinea, Indonesia, and Australia
Food: rodents, birds, bats, and marsupials
Method of hunting: a constrictor
Length: can reach 18 ft (6 m)